PIANO · VOCAL · GUITAR

ONE DIRECTION

TAKE ME HOME

ISBN 978-1-4803-2865-5

HAL•LEONARD® CORPORATION

7777 W. BLUEMOUND RD. P.O. BOX 13819 MILWAUKEE, WI 53213

Visit Hal Leonard Online at
www.halleonard.com

LIVE WHILE WE'RE YOUNG

Words and Music by RAMI YACOUB,
SAVAN KOTECHA and CARL FALK

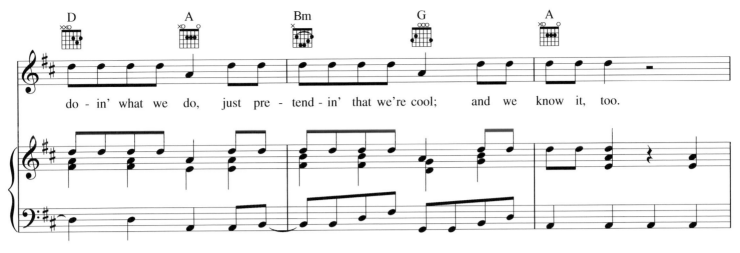

do - in' what we do, just pre - tend - in' that we're cool; and we know it, too.

Yeah, we'll keep do - in' what we do, just pre - tend - in' that we're cool. So to -

night, let's go cra - zy, cra - zy, cra - zy 'til we see the ___ sun. ___ I

know we on - ly met, but let's pre - tend it's ___ love ___ and nev - er, nev - er, nev - er stop for

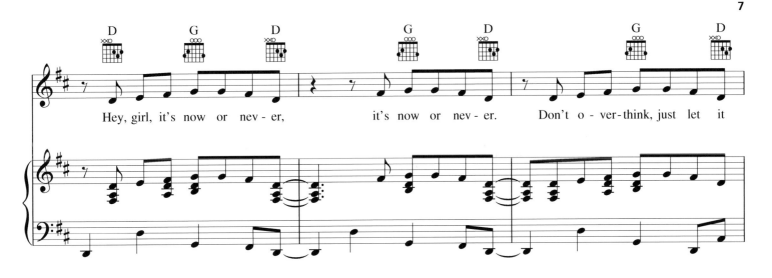

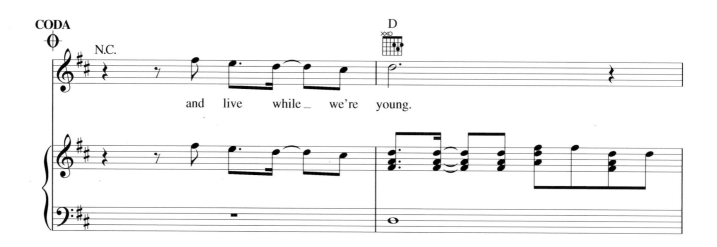

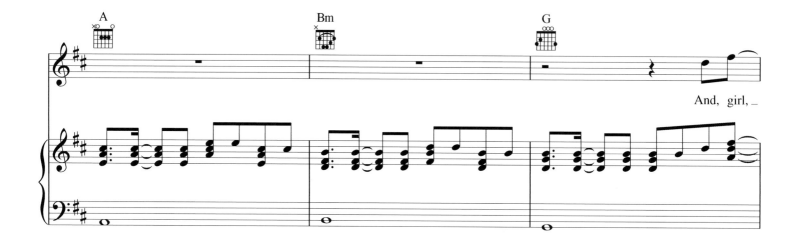

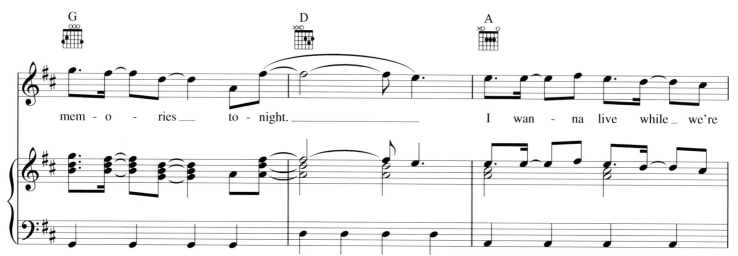

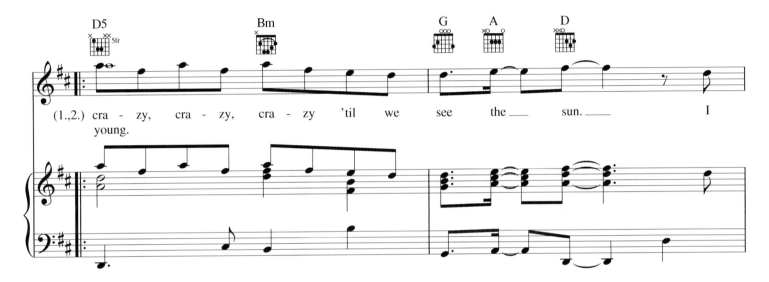

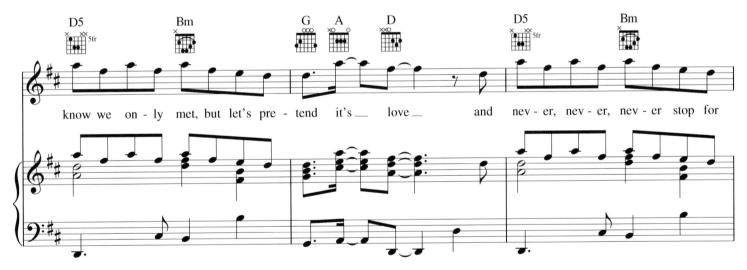

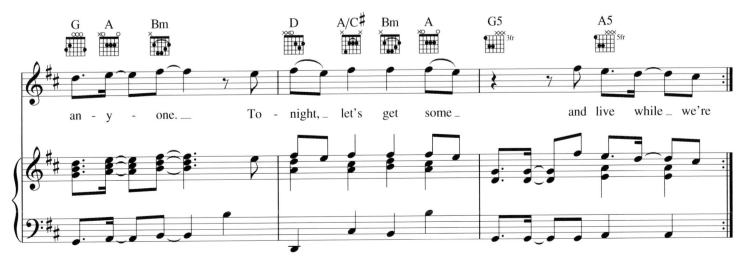

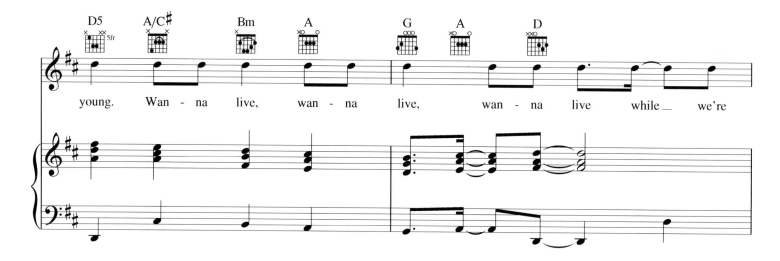

KISS YOU

Words and Music by SHELLBACK, SAVAN KOTECHA,
KRISTIAN LUNDIN, RAMI YACOUB, CARL FALK,
KRISTOFFER FOGELMARK and ALBIN NEDLER

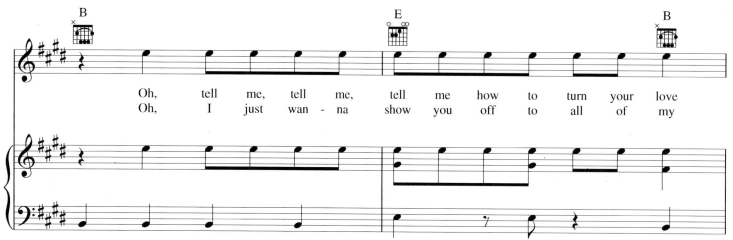

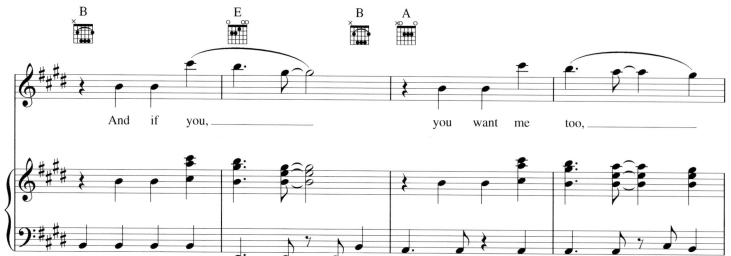

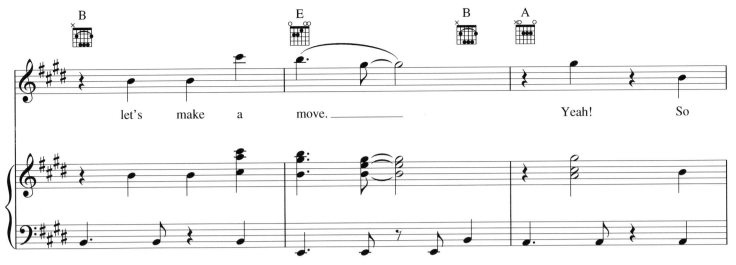

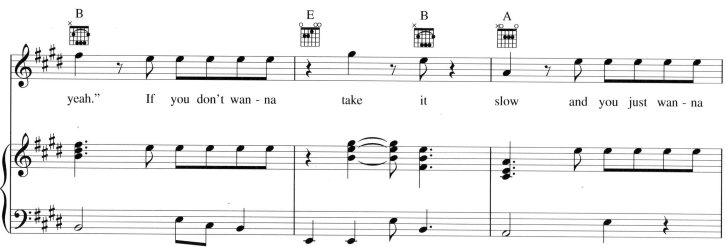

yeah." If you don't wan - na take it slow and you just wan - na

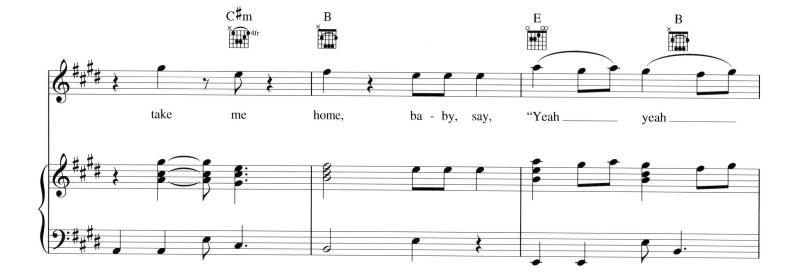

take me home, ba - by, say, "Yeah _____ yeah _____

yeah, _____ yeah _____ yeah," and let me kiss ___ you.

Oh, ba - by, ba - by, let me kiss ___ you.

(Let me kiss ___ you.)   (Let me kiss ___ you.)

(Let me kiss ___ you.)

(Let me kiss ___ you.) (Na, na, na na na na na, na. ___

LITTLE THINGS

Words and Music by ED SHEERAN
and FIONA BEVAN

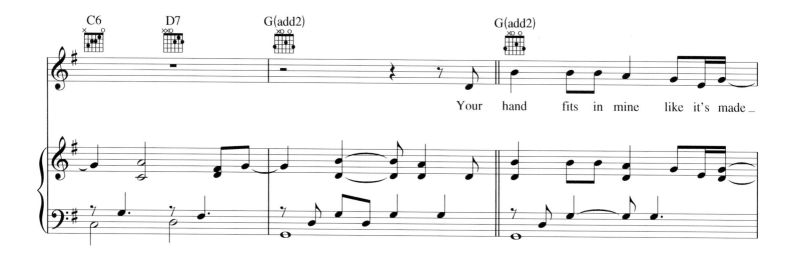

Your hand fits in mine like it's made _

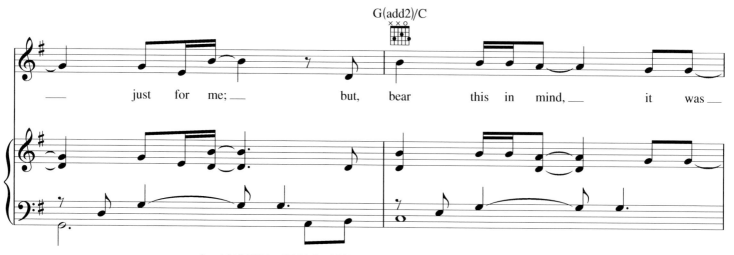

— just for me; _ but, bear this in mind, _ it was _

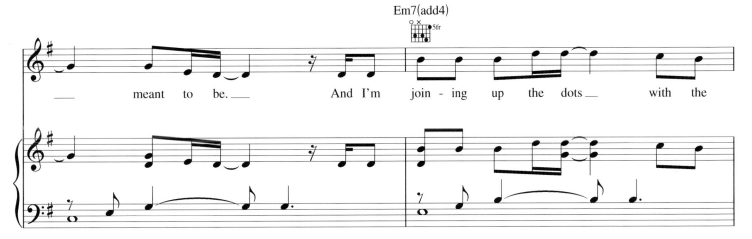

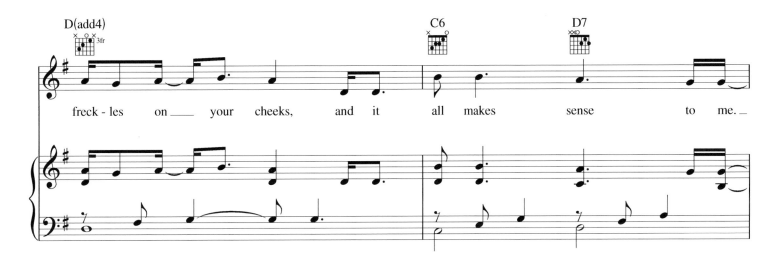

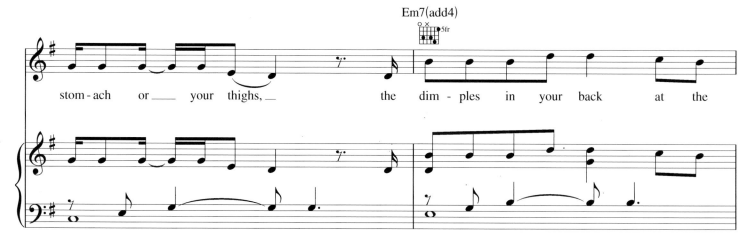

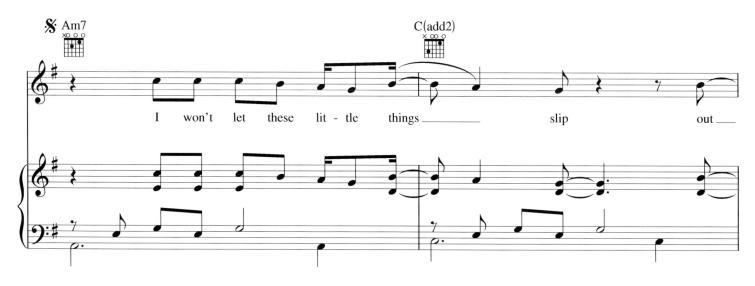

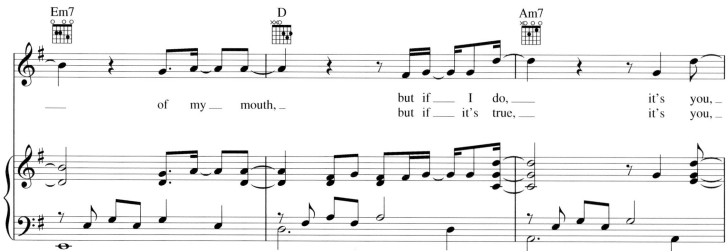

oh, it's you ___ that they __ add up to.
it's __ you ___ they __ add up to. I'm in __ love __

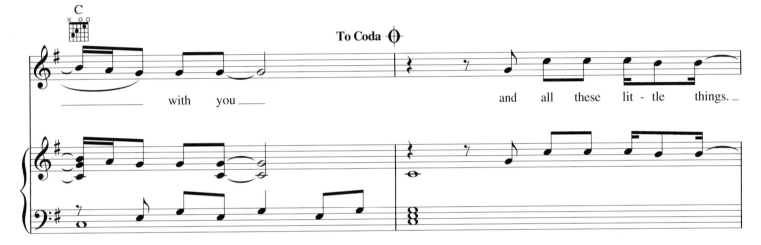

To Coda

_____ with you ___ and all these lit - tle things. __

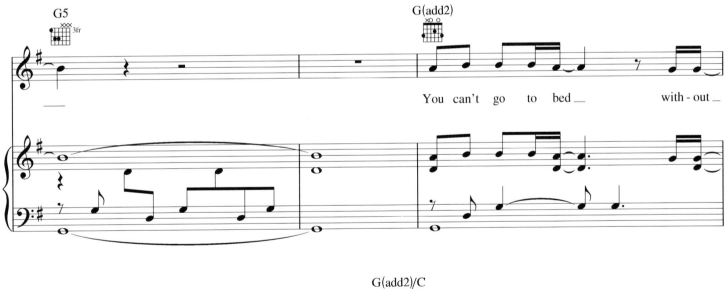

You can't go to bed __ with - out __

__ a cup of tea, __ and may - be that's the rea - son that you talk __

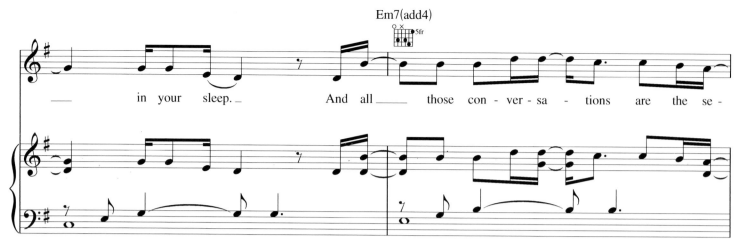

in your sleep. And all those con-ver-sa-tions are the se-

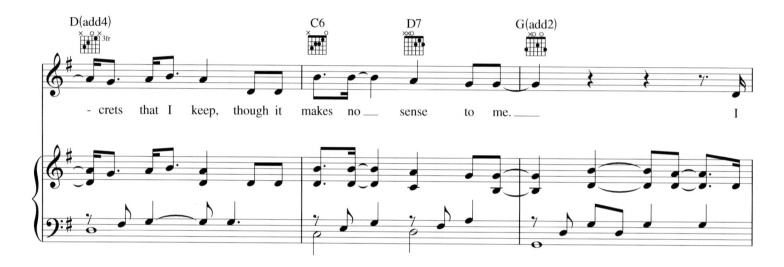

-crets that I keep, though it makes no sense to me. I

know you've nev-er loved the sound of your voice on tape.

You nev-er want to know how much you weigh.

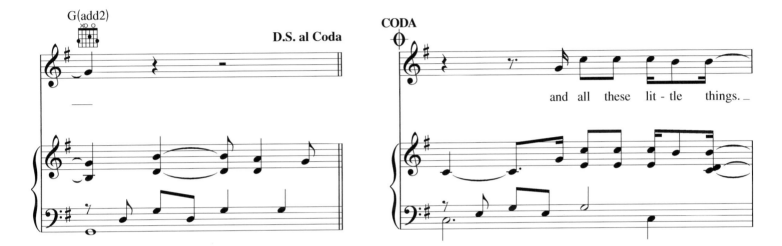

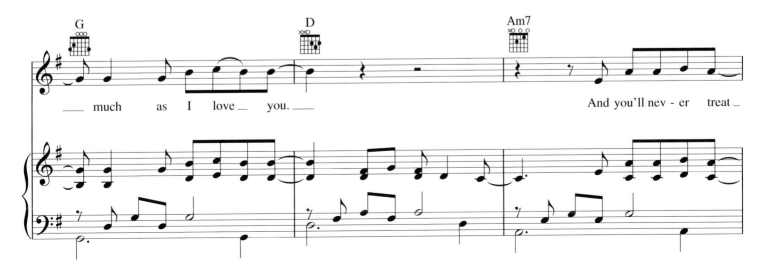

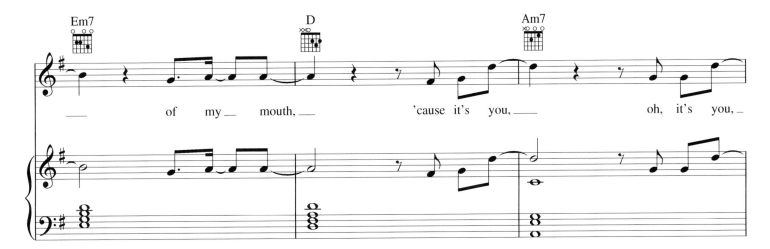

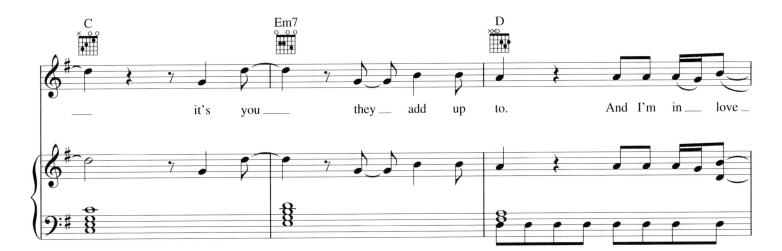

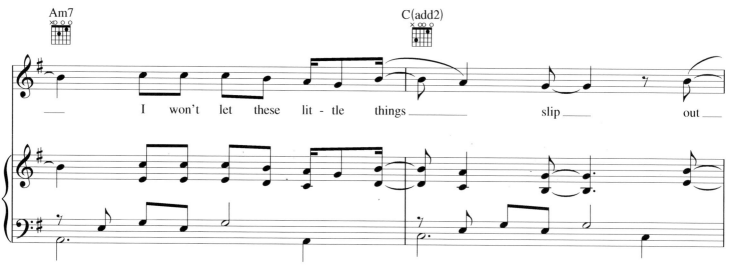

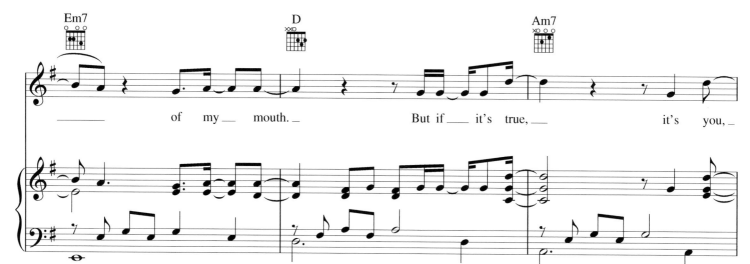

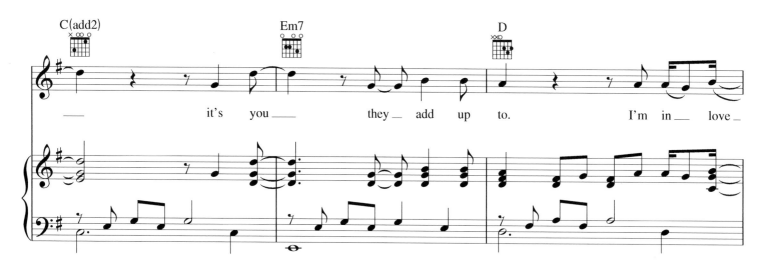

C'MON C'MON

Words and Music by JAMIE SCOTT,
JOHN RYAN and JULIAN BUNETTA

But you look a - maz - ing _____ stand-ing a - lone. _____
The way that you let your hair ____ down, _____ I can tell that you do. ____

_____ (So, c'- mon, c'- mon.) Move ____ a lit - tle clos - er, now.

(C'- mon, c'- mon.) Ain't ____ no way you're walk-ing out! (C'- mon, c'- mon.) Show ____

____ me what you're all a - bout. Yeah, I've been watch-ing you

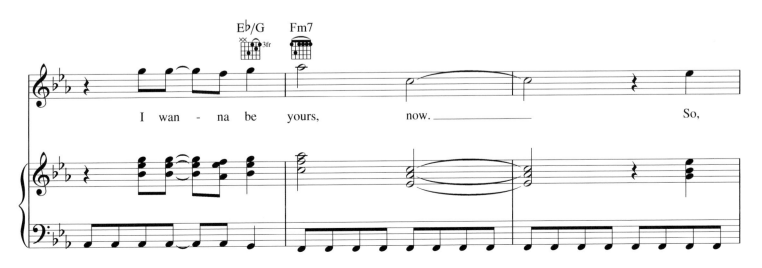

c'-mon, c'-mon and dance __ with me, ba - by. __ with me, ba - by.

Ev -'ry step I take, I'm feel-ing more and more, she is call-ing out;

she's a luck - y girl. _____ My __ heart is rac - ing; she is turn-ing a-round.

I reach for her hand, and I ____ say: Hey,

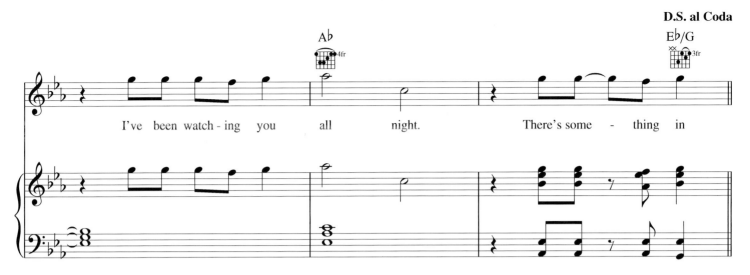

I've been watch-ing you all night. There's some - thing in

__ with me, ba - by.

(C' - mon, c' - mon.) (C' - mon, c' - mon.)

C' - mon, c' - mon and dance __ with me, ba - by.

LAST FIRST KISS

Words and Music by SAVAN KOTECHA, KRISTOFFER FOGELMARK,
ALBIN NEDLER, RAMI YACOUB, CARL FALK,
LIAM PAYNE, LOUIS TOMLINSON and ZAIN MALIK

first, yeah, wan-na be the first to take it all the way like this. And if

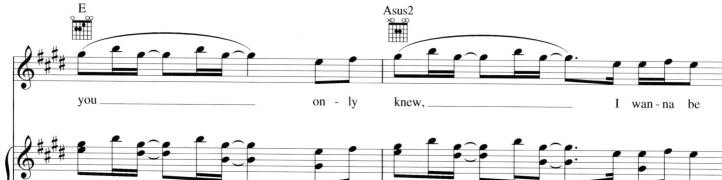

you _____ on-ly knew, _____ I wan-na be

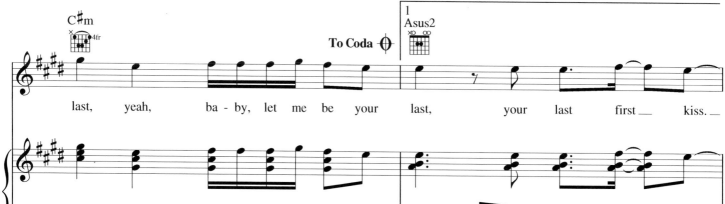

last, yeah, ba-by, let me be your last, your last first __ kiss. __

last, your last first __ kiss. __

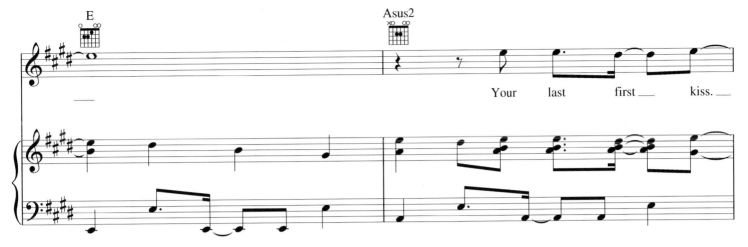

last, your last first kiss.

I wan-na be last, yeah, ba-by, let me be your

last, your last first kiss. I wan-na be

last, yeah, ba-by, let me be your last, your last first kiss.

HEART ATTACK

Words and Music by SHELLBACK,
SAVAN KOTECHA, KRISTIAN LUNDIN,
RAMI YACOUB and CARL FALK

(Yeah, yeah, yeah yeah yeah, yeah.)

Ba - by, you got me sick. I don't know what I did.
Ba - by, now that you're gone, I can't stand dumb love songs.

Need to take a break and fig - ure it out, yeah.
Miss - ing you is all I'm think - ing a - bout, yeah.

Got your voice in ___ my ___ head say - ing, "Let's just ___ be ___ friends."
Ev - 'ry - one's tell - ing ___ me I'm just too blind ___ to ___ see

Can't be - lieve the words came out of your mouth, yeah. I'm
how you messed me up; I'm bet - ter off now, yeah.

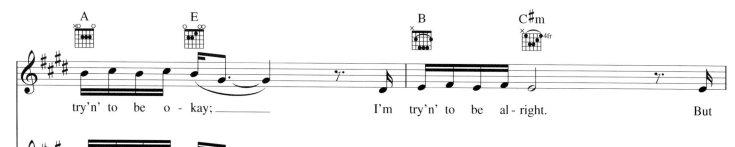

try'n' to be o - kay; ___ I'm try'n' to be al - right. But

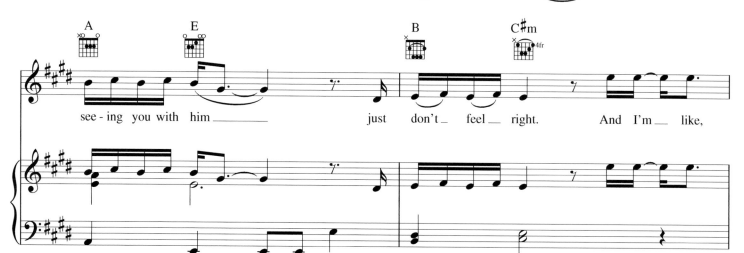

see - ing you with him ___ just don't ___ feel ___ right. And I'm ___ like,

ROCK ME

Words and Music by HENRY WALTER,
ALLAN GRIGG, PETER SVENSSON,
LUKASZ GOTTWALD and SAM HOLLANDER

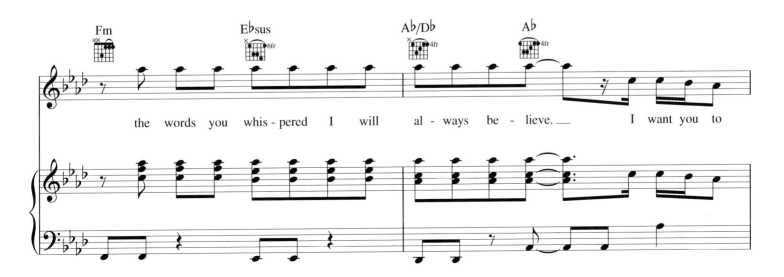

wan-na roll back like press-ing re-wind. You were mine and we nev-er ___ said good-

bye, _____ I, ___ I.

rock me, yeah. ___

R - O - C - K me a - gain, R - O - C - K me a - gain,

R - O - C - K me a - gain, yeah. ___ I want you to

gain, yeah. __ I want you to rock me, rock me, rock me, yeah. __ I want you to

L.H. tacet 1st time

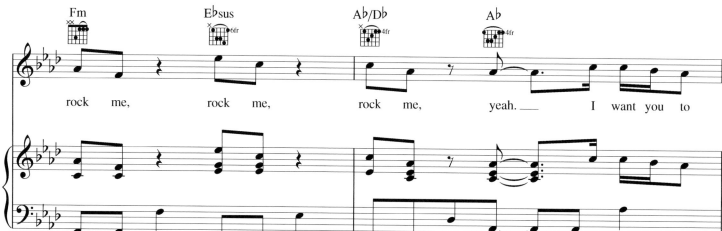

rock me, rock me, rock me, yeah. ___ I want you to

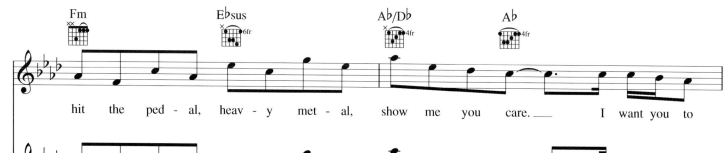

hit the ped - al, heav - y met - al, show me you care. ___ I want you to

Play L.H. both times

rock me, rock me, rock me, yeah. __ I want you to rock me, yeah. __

CHANGE MY MIND

Words and Music by SAVAN KOTECHA,
RAMI YACOUB and CARL FALK

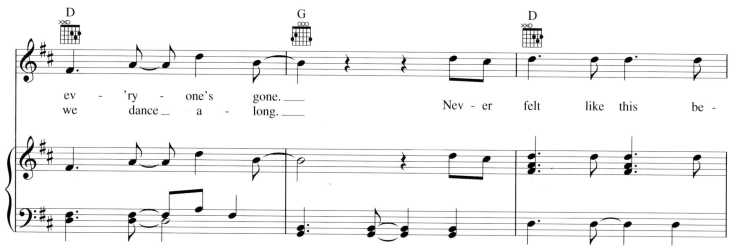

ev - 'ry - one's gone.___
we dance___ a - long.___ Nev - er felt like this be -

fore;_____ are we friends, or are we more?_____ As I'm

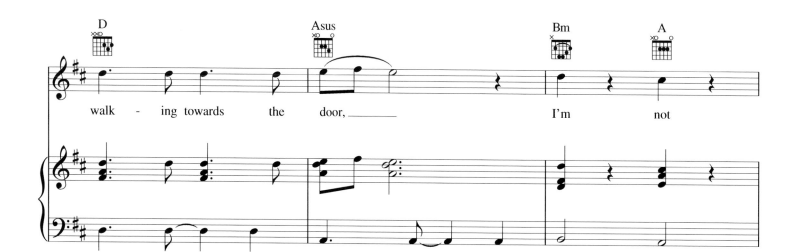

walk - ing towards the door,_____ I'm not

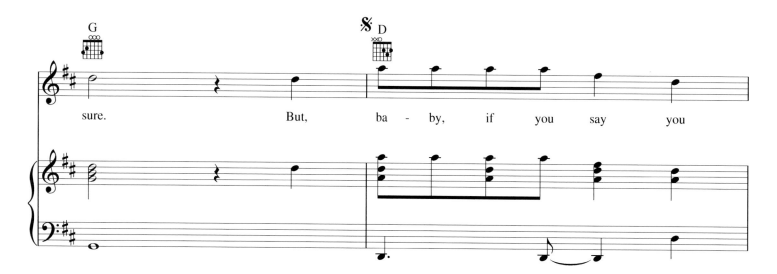

sure. But, ba - by, if you say you

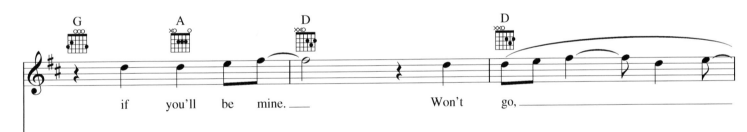

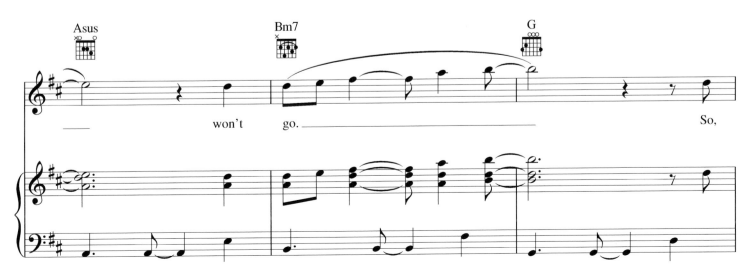

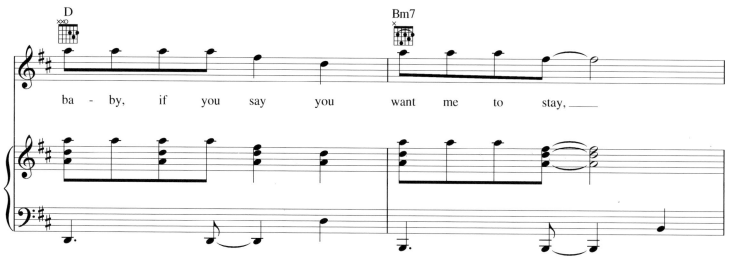

ba - by, if you say you want me to stay, _____

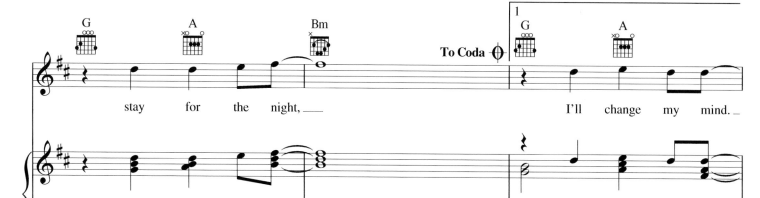

stay for the night, _____ I'll change my mind. _____

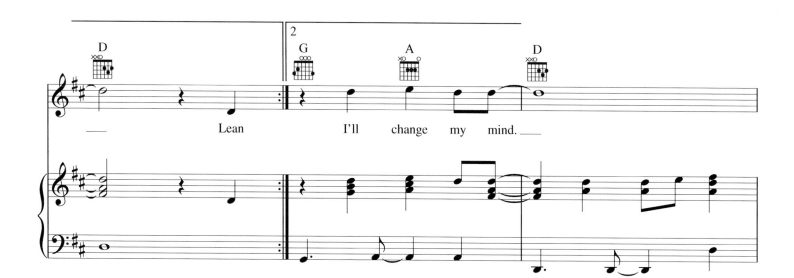

Lean I'll change my mind. _____

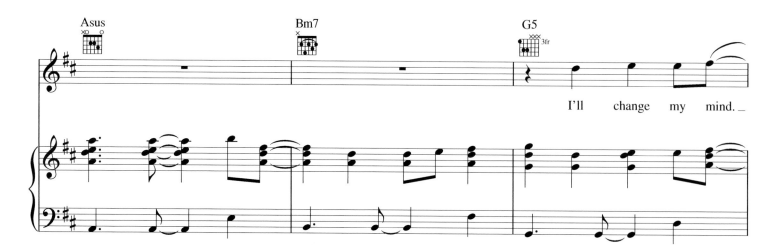

I'll change my mind. _____

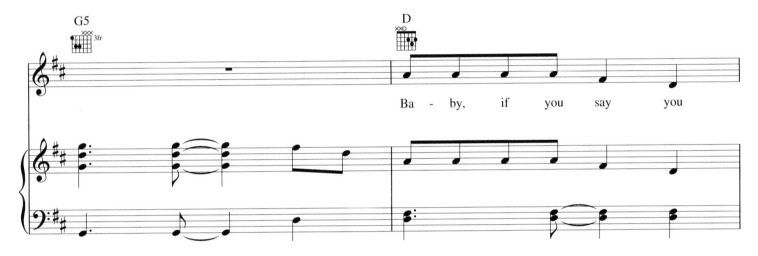

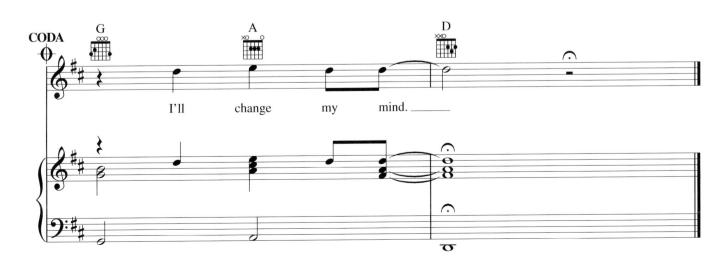

I WOULD

Words and Music by THOMAS FLETCHER,
DAN JONES and DOUGIE POYNTER

one thing __ you've al - read - y got.
al - i - ty ru - ined __ my life.
It

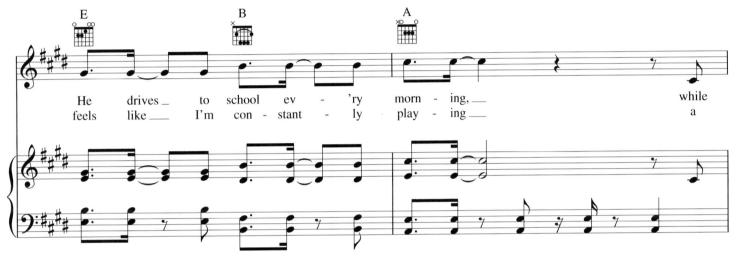

He drives __ to school ev - 'ry morn - ing, __
feels like __ I'm con - stant - ly play - ing __
while
a

I walk a - lone in __ the rain.
game that __ I'm des - tined __ to lose,
He'd
'cause

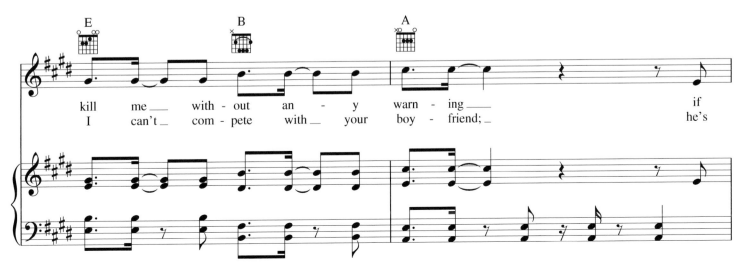

kill me __ with - out an - y warn - ing __
I can't __ com - pete with __ your boy - friend; __
if
he's

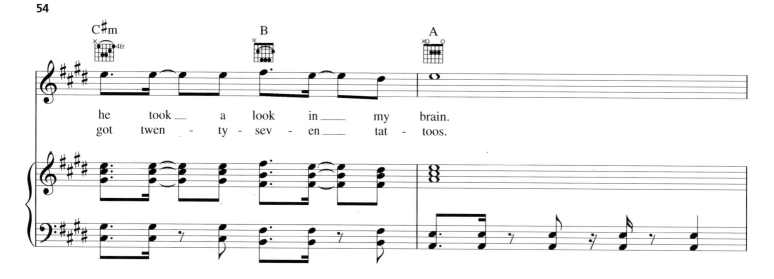

he took ___ a look in ___ my brain.
got twen - ty - sev - en ___ tat - toos.

Would he say he's in L - O - V - E? ___ Well, if

it was ___ me, ___ then I would. (I would.) ___ Would he hold you when you're

feel - ing ___ low? ___ Ba - by, you should ___ know ___ that I

55

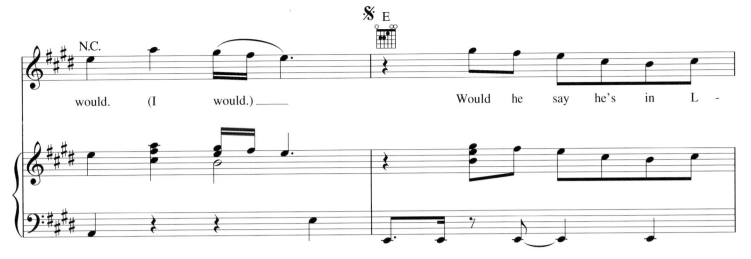

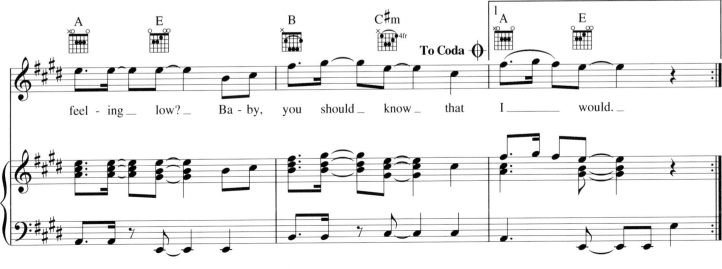

I _____ would. __ (I _____ would.) __ (I _____ would.) __

Would he please __ you? Would he kiss __ you?

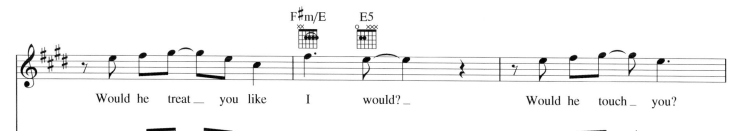

Would he treat __ you like I would? _ Would he touch __ you?

Would he need __ you? Would he love __ you like I _____ would? _

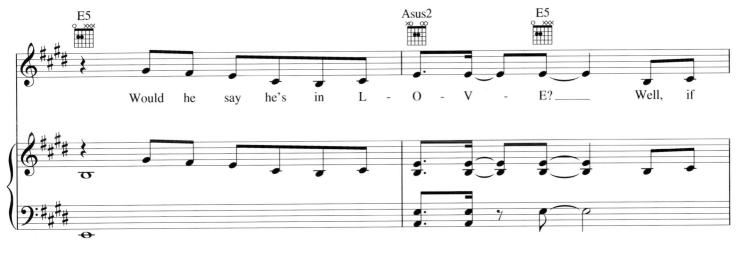

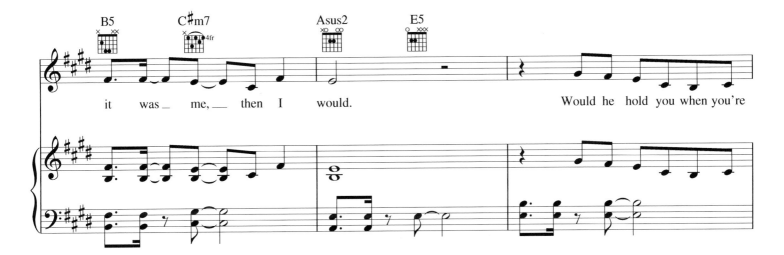

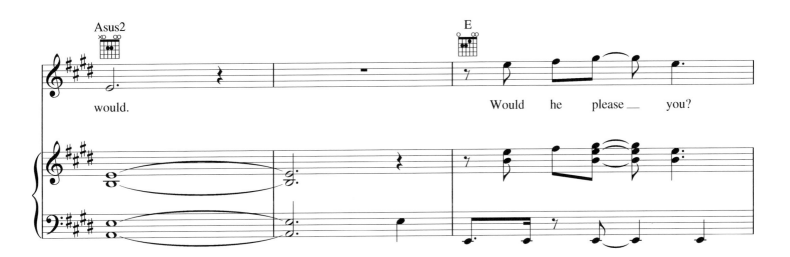

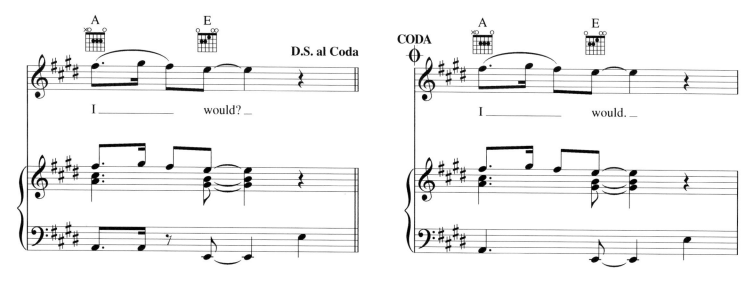

OVER AGAIN

Words and Music by ED SHEERAN,
ALEX GOWERS and ROBERT CONLON

Bod - ies in - ter - twine with her lips. Now she's feel - ing

so low since she went so - lo; hole in the mid - dle of my heart like a

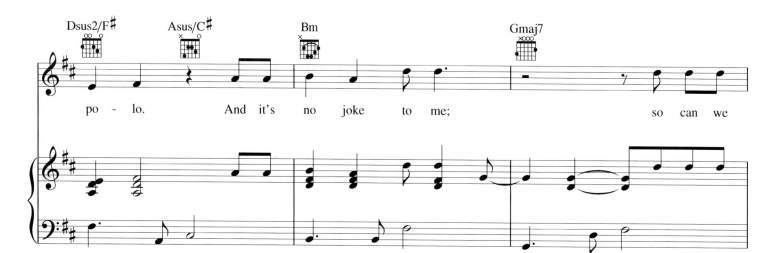

po - lo. And it's no joke to me; so can we

do it all o - ver a - gain? (If you're pre -

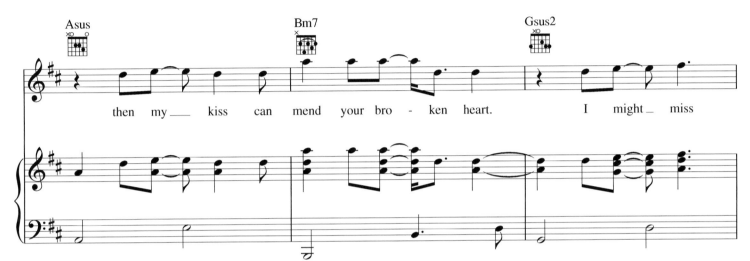

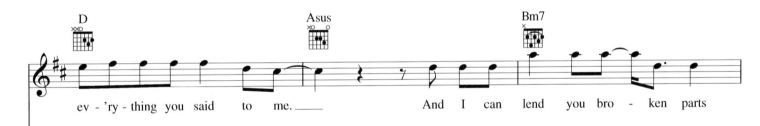

To Coda

give you all ___ my heart _____ so we can

start it all o - ver a - gain.) Can we take the same road,

two days in the same clothes? And I know just what she'll say if I can

make all this pain ___ go. ___ Can we stop ___ this for a

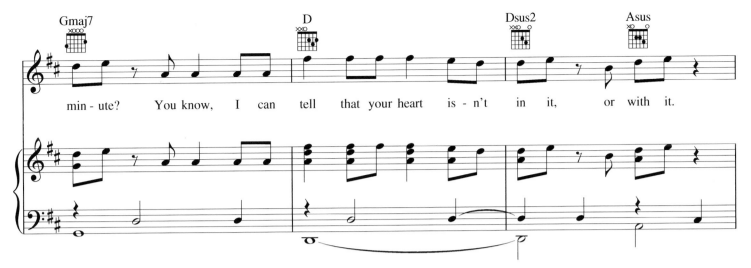

min - ute? You know, I can tell that your heart is - n't in it, or with it.

Tell me with your mind, bod - y and spir - it. I can make your

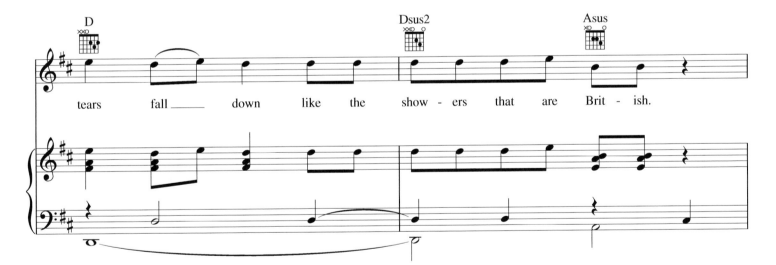

tears fall _____ down like the show - ers that are Brit - ish.

Wheth - er we're to - geth - er or a - part, we can both re - move the

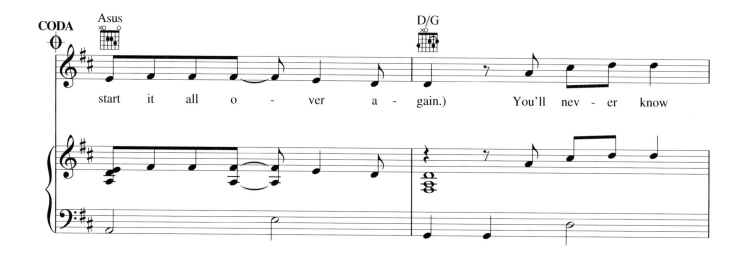

do you real - ly want to be a - lone? If you're pre -

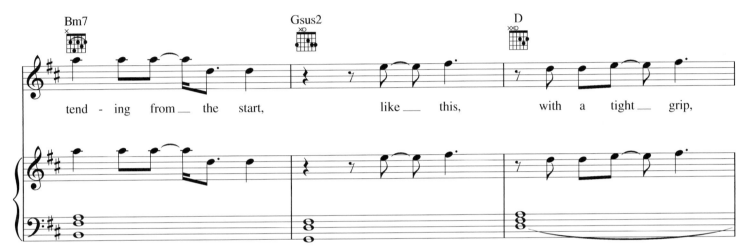

tend - ing from __ the start, like __ this, with a tight __ grip,

then my __ kiss can mend your bro - ken heart. I might __ miss

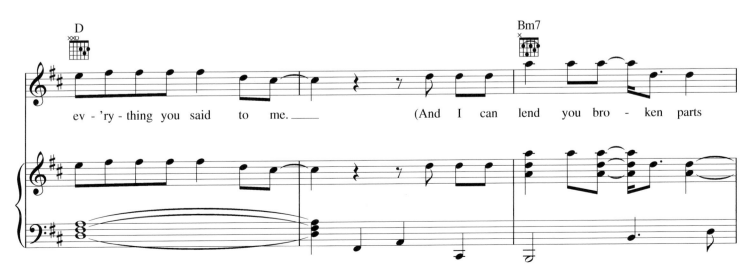

ev - 'ry - thing you said to me. ___ (And I can lend you bro - ken parts

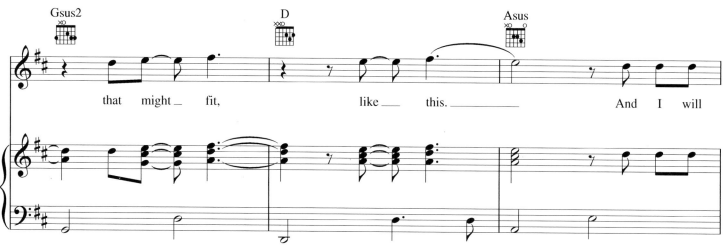

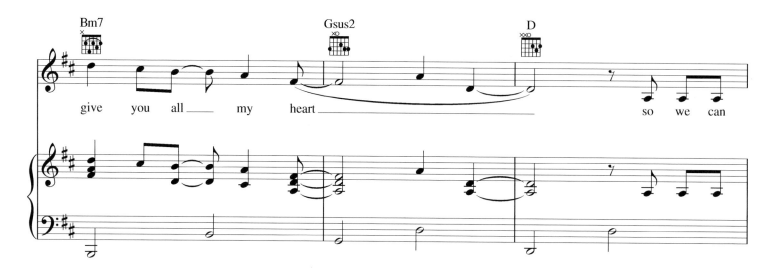

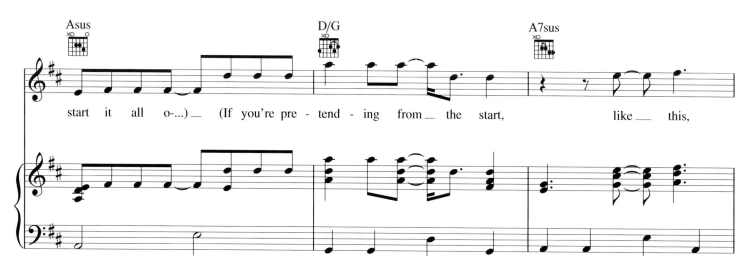

I might _ miss ev - 'ry - thing you said to me. _ And I can

lend you bro - ken parts that might _ fit, like _ this. _

_ And I will give you all _ my heart...) _

...so we can start it all o - ver a - gain.

BACK FOR YOU

Words and Music by SAVAN KOTECHA,
KRISTOFFER FOGELMARK, ALBIN NEDLER, RAMI YACOUB,
CARL FALK, LIAM PAYNE, LOUIS TOMLINSON,
HARRY STYLES and NIALL HORAN

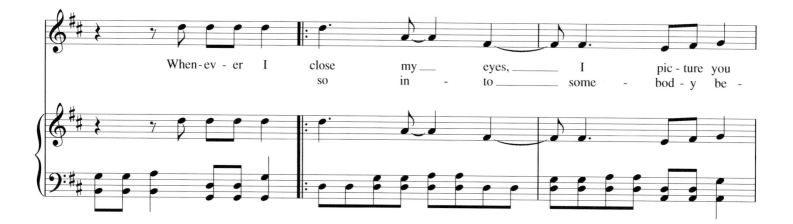

from the stage, _____ yeah; your smile is on
gon - na change, _____ yeah, and you won't ev - er

ev - 'ry face, _____ now. But ev -'ry time you wake __ up, _____
walk a - way, _____ yeah. 'Cause e - ven though ev - 'ry ___ night, ___

__ you're hear - ing me say, "Good - bye." _____
__ you'll know what I'll say: "Good - bye," _____

D5   A5   B5   G5

(1.,3.) Ba - by, you don't have __ to wor - ry;
(2.) ba - by,

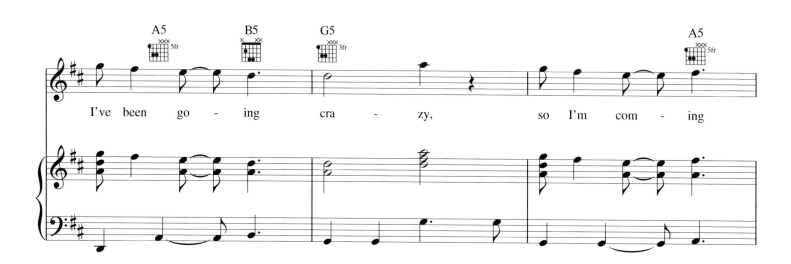

you. _____

I've nev - er been

Right back for you, _____ whoa. _____

you. _____

_____ Right back for you, _____ right back for you. _____

_____ Late - ly,

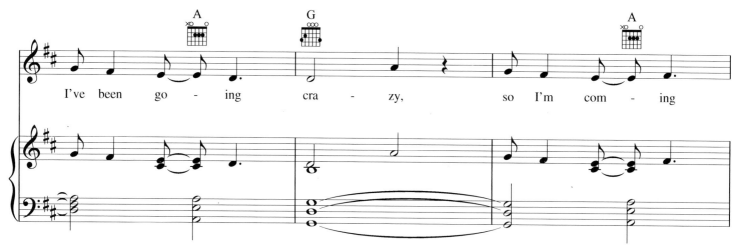

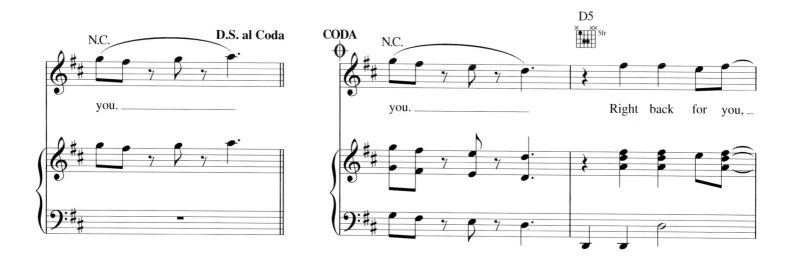

Right back for you, _____ right back. Right back for _____

you. _____ Late - ly, I've been go - ing

cra - zy, so I'm com - ing back for you,

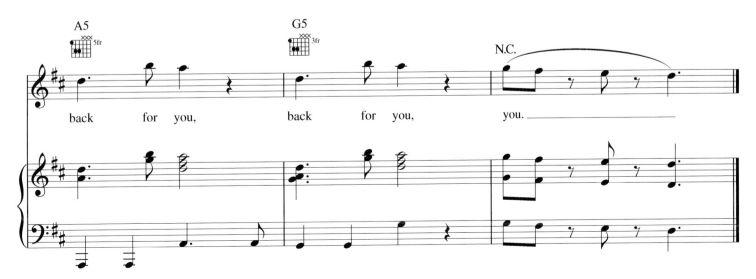

back for you, back for you, you. _____

THEY DON'T KNOW ABOUT US

Words and Music by PETER WALLEVIK,
TOMMY LEE JAMES, TEBEY OTTOH
and TOMMY P. GREGERSEN

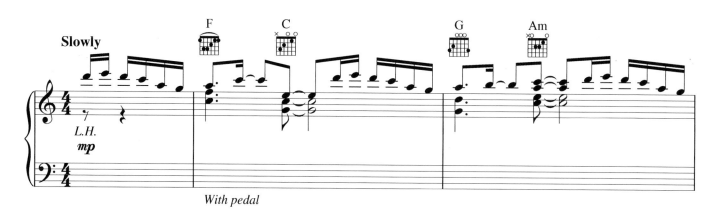

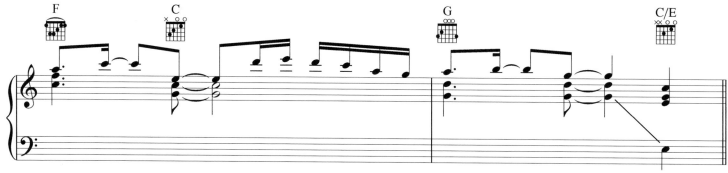

Peo-ple say we should-n't be to-geth-er, too young to know a-bout for-ev-er.

But I say, they don't know what they're talk-talk-talk-ing a-bout. _

(Talk-talk-talk-ing a-bout.) _

just be jeal-ous of us. They don't know a-bout the up - all - nights. They don't know I've wait-ed

all my ___ life just to find a love that feels this ___ right. Ba - by,

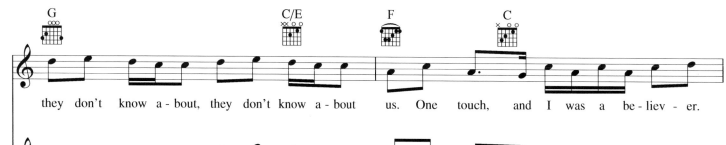

they don't know a - bout, they don't know a-bout us. One touch, and I was a be - liev - er.

Ev-'ry kiss, it gets a lit-tle sweet-er. It's get-ting bet-ter, keeps_ get-ting bet-ter all the

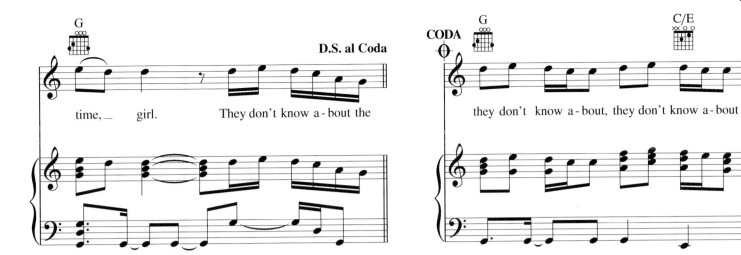

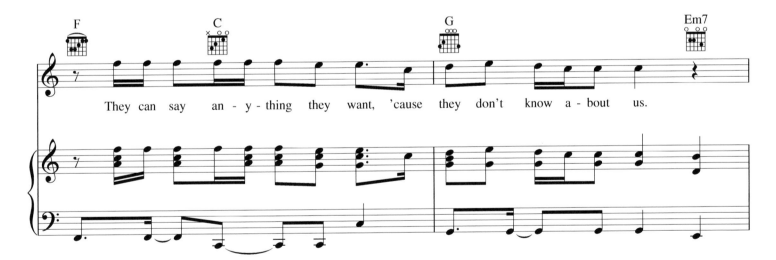

all my __ life just to find a love that feels this __ right. Ba - by,

they don't know a - bout us. They don't know a - bout the
(They don't know a - bout...)

they don't know a - bout us, a - bout _____ us.
(They don't know a - bout us.)

They don't know a - bout __ us.

SUMMER LOVE

Words and Music by LINDY ROBBINS, WAYNE HECTOR,
STEVE ROBSON, LIAM PAYNE, LOUIS TOMLINSON,
ZAIN MALIK, HARRY STYLES and NIALL HORAN

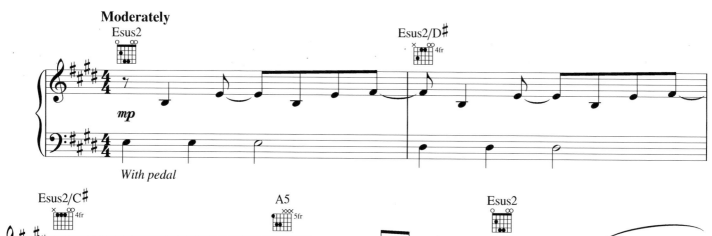

Yeah. ___ Ooh.

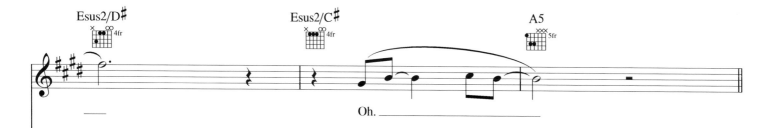

Oh.

Can't be-lieve ___ you're   pack-ing your ___ bags,
Wish that we ___ could   be a-lone ___ now,

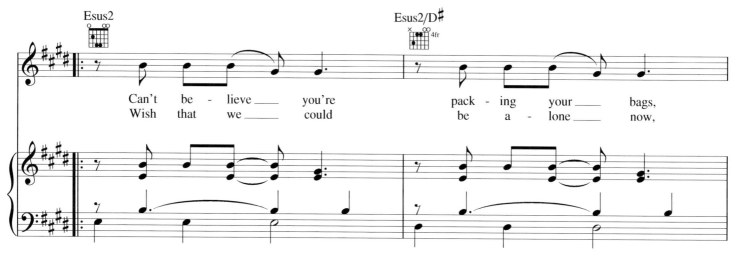

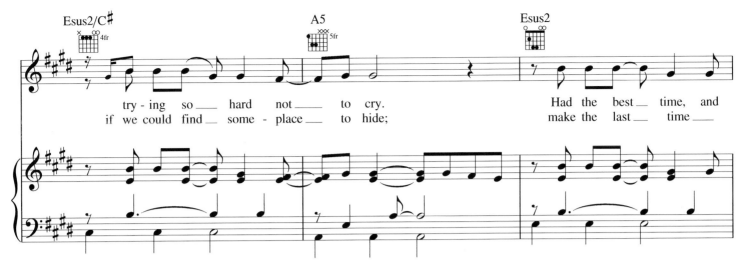

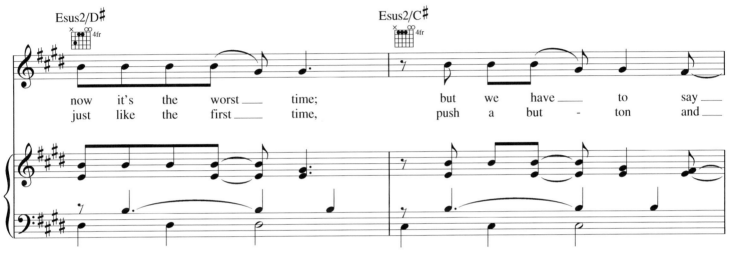

Just prom - ise that you won't ___ for - get ___ we
Just prom - ise you'll re - mem - ber when ___ the ___

had ___ it all. ___ 'Cause you were mine ___ for the sum -
sky ___ is gray. ___

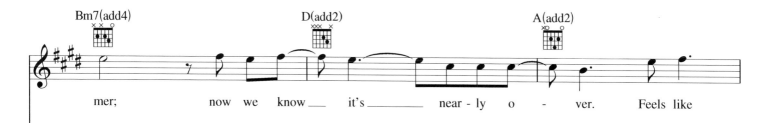

mer; now we know ___ it's ___ near - ly o - ver. Feels like

snow ___ in Sep - tem - ber, but I al - ways ___ will re - mem -

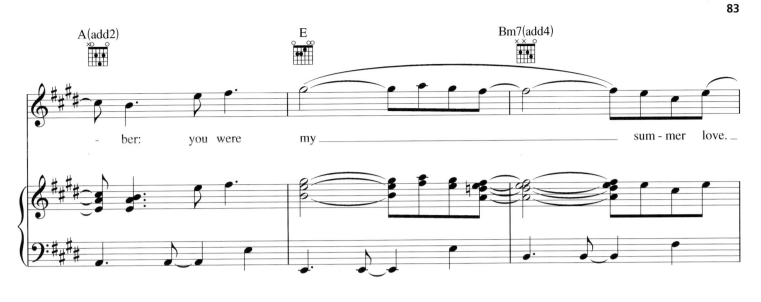

-ber: you were my _____ sum-mer love. _____

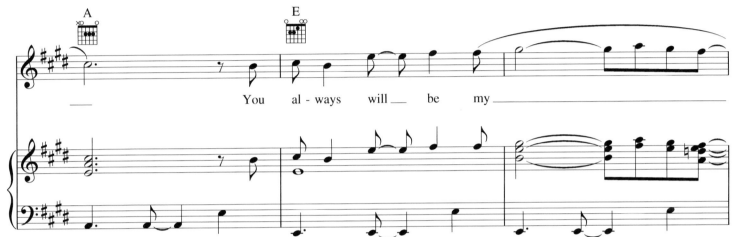

You al-ways will __ be my _____

sum-mer love. _____

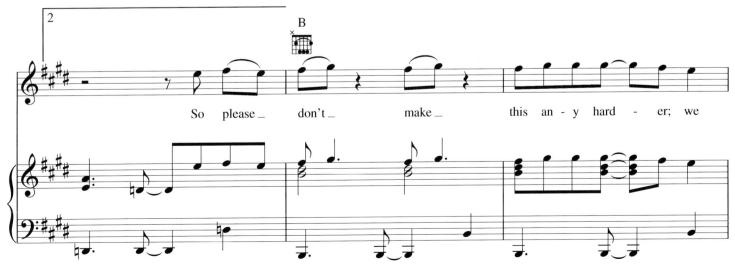

So please __ don't __ make __ this an-y hard-er; we

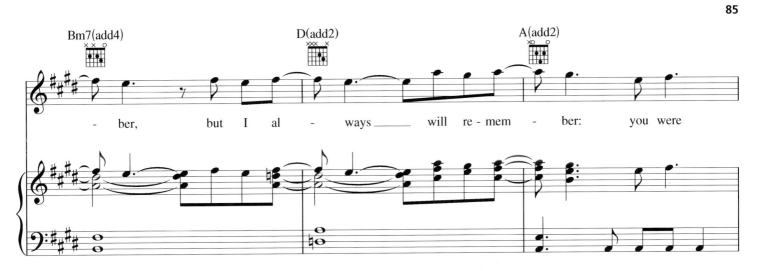

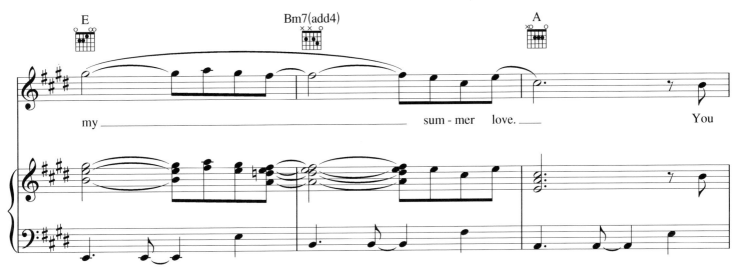

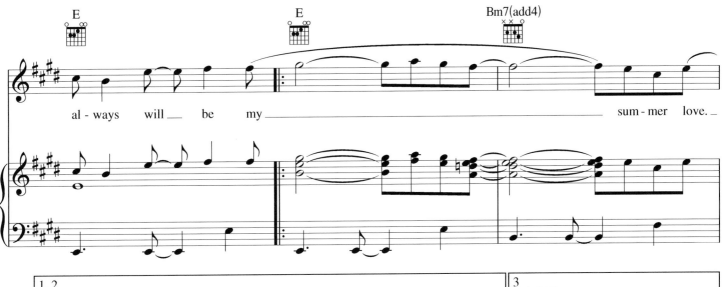

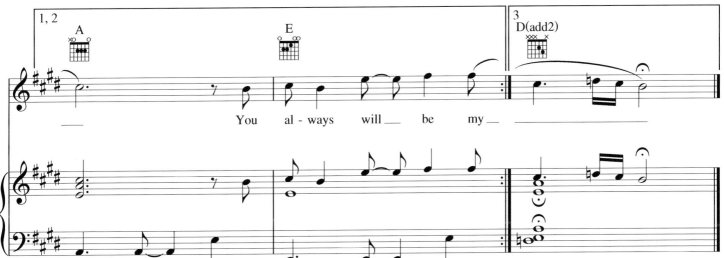